LOOK AT U.S. HISTORY

THE GETTYSBURG ADDRESS

BY BEATRICE HARRIS

Gareth Stevens PUBLISHING

CRASHCOURSE

Please visit our website, www.garethstevens.com. For a free color catalog of all our high-quality books, call toll free 1-800-542-2595 or fax 1-877-542-2596.

Cataloging-in-Publication Data

Names: Harris, Beatrice.
Title: The Gettysburg Address / Beatrice Harris.
Description: New York : Gareth Stevens Publishing, 2022. | Series: A look at U.S. history | Includes glossary and index.
Identifiers: ISBN 9781538266410 (pbk.) | ISBN 9781538266434 (library bound) | ISBN 9781538266427 (6 pack) | ISBN 9781538266441 (ebook)
Subjects: LCSH: Lincoln, Abraham, 1809-1865. Gettysburg address--Juvenile literature. | Lincoln, Abraham, 1809-1865. Gettysburg address. | Gettysburg address (Lincoln, Abraham).
Classification: LCC E475.55 H1767 2022 | DDC 973.7'349--dc23

First Edition

Published in 2022 by
Gareth Stevens Publishing
111 East 14th Street, Suite 349
New York, NY 10003

Editor: Therese Shea

Photo credits: Series art Christophe BOISSON/Shutterstock.com; (feather quill) Galushko Sergey/Shutterstock.com; (parchment) mollicart-design/Shutterstock.com; cover, p. 1 courtesy of the Library of Congress; pp. 5, 23 (bottom) Universal History Archive/Universal Images Group via Getty Images; p. 7 Keith Lance/ DigitalVision Vectors/Getty Images; p. 9 MPI/ Getty Images; p. 11 AnthonySchafer/ iStock / Getty Images Plus; p. 13 Stock Montage/Getty Images; p. 15 traveler1116/ DigitalVision Vectors/Getty Images; p. 17 Craig Fildes/Moment/ Getty Images; p. 19 Bettmann/Getty Images; p. 21 Sepia Times/Universal Images Group via Getty Images; p. 23 (top) Stefani Reynolds/Bloomberg via Getty Images; p. 25 (top) Bernard Hoffman/The LIFE Picture Collection via Getty Images; p. 25 (bottom) Library Of Congress/ Getty Images; p. 27 John Parrot/Stocktrek Images/Getty Images; p. 29 CaptLensCap/ iStock / Getty Images Plus.

Printed in the United States of America

CPSIA compliance information: Batch #CSGS22: For further information contact Gareth Stevens, New York, New York at 1-800-542-2595.

CONTENTS

Words in the glossary appear in **bold** type the first time they are used in the text.

TALKING HISTORY

"Four score and seven years ago . . ." Have you ever heard these words? Maybe you know they're the beginning words of the Gettysburg Address. But do you know why this address, or speech, is so famous? Read on to find out!

THE GETTYSBURG ADDRESS

DELIVERED BY ABRAHAM LINCOLN NOV. 19 1863

AT THE DEDICATION SERVICES ON THE BATTLE FIELD

Four score and seven years ago our fathers brought forth on this continent a new nation, conceived in liberty, and dedicated to the proposition that all men are created equal. Now we are engaged in a great civil war, testing whether that nation, or any nation so conceived and so dedicated, can long endure. We are met on a great battle-field of that war. We have come to dedicate a portion of that field as a final resting place for those who here gave their lives that that nation might live. It is altogether fitting and proper that we should do this. But in a larger sense we cannot dedicate, we cannot consecrate, we cannot hallow this ground. The brave men, living and dead, who struggled here, have consecrated it far above our poor power to add or detract. The world will little note, nor long remember, what we say here, but it can never forget what they did here. It is for us, the living, rather to be dedicated here to the unfinished work which they who fought here have thus far so nobly advanced. It is rather for us to be here dedicated to the great task remaining before us, that from these honored dead we take increased devotion to that cause for which they gave the last full measure of devotion; that we here highly resolve that these dead shall not have died in vain; that this nation, under God, shall have a new birth of freedom, and that the government of the people, by the people, and for the people, shall not perish from the earth

MAKE THE GRADE

There are just 272 words in the Gettysburg Address.

THE AMERICAN CIVIL WAR

The Gettysburg Address was given during the American Civil War. This war was fought from 1861 to 1865. It began after the Southern states broke away from the rest of the United States. They formed a country called the Confederate States of America.

MAKE THE GRADE

Slavery was the main cause of the Civil War. The South feared that the U.S. government under President Abraham Lincoln would end slavery and harm the Southern way of life.

THE BATTLE OF GETTYSBURG

The bloodiest battle of the Civil War was in Gettysburg, Pennsylvania. It was fought from July 1 to July 3, 1863. Confederate soldiers under General Robert E. Lee were **invading** the North. However, **Union** troops under General George Meade stopped them.

MAKE THE GRADE

The Battle of Gettysburg was called the turning point of the Civil War. The Union stopped the Confederate invasion of the North. The Confederate army was never as strong again.

A CEMETERY'S DEDICATION

Many soldiers lost their lives during the Battle of Gettysburg. A **cemetery** was planned for the Union soldiers who had died. The **dedication** of the cemetery took place on November 19, 1863. Famous people were asked to take part.

MAKE THE GRADE

During the Battle of Gettysburg, about 23,000 Union soldiers and 28,000 Confederate soldiers were killed or harmed.

The man in charge of setting up the cemetery was named David Wills. He asked an orator, or speaker, named Edward Everett to give the main speech. Wills asked President Abraham Lincoln to give a short speech too.

MAKE THE GRADE

Edward Everett spoke for about two hours before Lincoln's speech.

LINCOLN SPEAKS

After Everett's speech, President Lincoln gave his Gettysburg Address. He began by talking of the nation's founding "four score and seven years ago," which means 1776. He said the country had been "dedicated to the **proposition** that all men are created equal."

MAKE THE GRADE

The word "score" in the first words of the Gettysburg Address means "20." So, "four score and seven years ago" is the same as 87 years before 1863, or 1776.

Lincoln said the war was testing if the United States, founded on the ideas of freedom and equality, could last. He stated it was "fitting and **proper**" for people to dedicate part of a battlefield to soldiers who had fought for the nation.

MAKE THE GRADE

Lincoln said Soldiers' National Cemetery in Gettysburg was "a final resting place for those who here gave their lives" so that the United States might live on.

Lincoln said, "The world will little note, nor long remember what we say here, but it can never forget what they [the soldiers] did here." He called on the nation to finish the "great task" the soldiers had fought for in battle.

MAKE THE GRADE

Mathew Brady was one of the first **photographers**. He took many photos during the Civil War, including this photo of Lincoln giving the Gettysburg Address.

Lincoln asked Americans to resolve, or decide, that the dead of the Civil War didn't die for nothing. If the North won the Civil War, he said, "this nation, under God, shall have a new birth of freedom."

MAKE THE GRADE

In 1863, under Lincoln's order called the Emancipation Proclamation, **enslaved** people in some Southern states were freed. Many didn't know until the Union soldiers arrived.

Lincoln finished his speech by saying that the Civil War was being fought so "government of the people, by the people, for the people, shall not **perish** from the earth." With these words, he reminded Americans that their nation was a **democracy**.

MAKE THE GRADE

"Government of the people, by the people, for the people" means American citizens run the U.S. government. It was made by them and for them too.

AFTER THE ADDRESS

Lincoln stopped speaking five times because people were clapping so much. Edward Everett later wrote to Lincoln, "I wish . . . that I had come as near to the central [main] idea of the **occasion**, in two hours, as you did in two minutes."

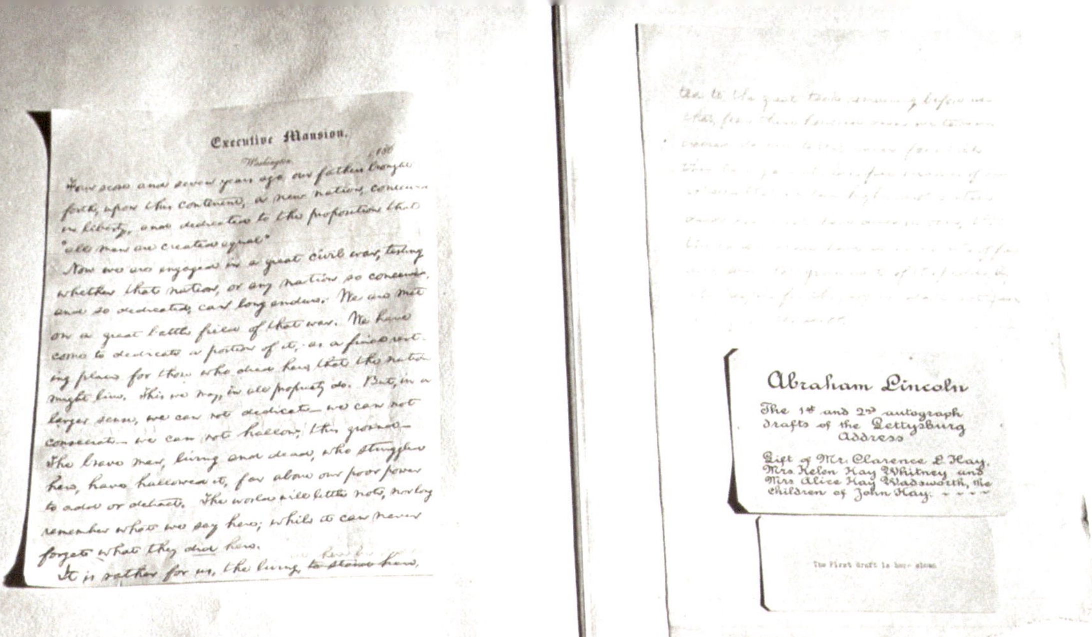

MAKE THE GRADE

There are five copies of Lincoln's Gettysburg Address in the president's handwriting. One is shown above.

With his address, Abraham Lincoln made people believe the Civil War was needed to **preserve** the nation. He also made them believe equality and freedom for all were important to the **foundation** of the country. They were worth fighting for.

MAKE THE GRADE

President Lincoln was shot on April 14, 1865,
near the end of the Civil War.
He died the next day.

LONG REMEMBERED

In the Gettysburg Address, Lincoln said, "The world will little note, nor long remember what we say here." However, people do remember. The speech changed how many thought of the nation and what it stands for. Americans still fight for freedom and equality today.

MAKE THE GRADE

In 1865, the Thirteenth **Amendment** banned slavery in all parts of the United States.

A SHORT TIMELINE OF THE CIVIL WAR

NOVEMBER 6, 1860
Abraham Lincoln is chosen to be president.

DECEMBER 20, 1860
South Carolina is the first state to leave the Union.

APRIL 12, 1861
The Civil War begins.

JULY 21, 1861
The Confederates win the First Battle of Bull Run.

SEPTEMBER 17, 1862
The Battle of Antietam becomes the deadliest battle in U.S. history up to that point.

JANUARY 1, 1863
The Emancipation Proclamation frees enslaved people in Confederate areas.

JULY 1, 1863
The Battle of Gettysburg begins.

JULY 3, 1863
The Union wins the Battle of Gettysburg.

NOVEMBER 19, 1863
Lincoln gives the Gettysburg Address.

SEPTEMBER 2, 1864
The Union takes Atlanta, Georgia.

NOVEMBER 15, 1864
The Union's March to the Sea across Georgia begins.

APRIL 9, 1865
Robert E. Lee gives up his Confederate army.

APRIL 14, 1865
Abraham Lincoln is shot.

APRIL 15, 1865
Lincoln dies.

GLOSSARY

amendment: a change or addition to a constitution, which is a nation's highest law

cemetery: a place where the dead are buried

dedication: an event to mark something's completion

democracy: the free and equal right of every person to participate in a government

enslaved: being owned by another person and forced to work without pay

foundation: something, such as an idea or a fact, that gives support for something

invade: to enter a place in order to take it over

occasion: a special time

perish: to come to an end

photographer: a person who takes pictures with a camera

preserve: to keep something in its original state

proper: correct

proposition: an idea to be tested, explained, or proven

Union: the side of the Northern states in the American Civil War

FOR MORE INFORMATION

Books

Miller, Mirella S. *12 Questions About the Gettysburg Address.* Mankato, MN: 12-Story Library, 2016.

Sjonger, Rebecca. *Abraham Lincoln: The Gettysburg Address.* New York, NY: Crabtree Publishing, 2019.

Websites

The Gettysburg Address
www.ushistory.org/documents/gettysburg.htm
Read the whole speech and see a copy up close.

Gettysburg Address: 1863
bensguide.gpo.gov/gettysburg-address-1863
Discover something new about the famous speech.

INDEX